Even Time Bleeds

THE LOCKERT LIBRARY OF POETRY IN TRANSLATION

SERIES EDITORS
Peter Cole, Richard Sieburth, and Rosanna Warren

SERIES EDITOR EMERITUS (1991–2016)
Richard Howard

For other titles in the Lockert Library, see the list at the end of this volume.

Even Time Bleeds

SELECTED POEMS

Jeannette L. Clariond
Translated and introduced by Forrest Gander

PRINCETON UNIVERSITY PRESS

PRINCETON AND OXFORD

The epigraph for "Anselm Kiefer me escucha / Anselm Kiefer Hears Me Out" is an excerpt of "Sprich auch du" from *Von Schwelle zu Schwelle* by Paul Celan. Published by Deutsche Verlags-Anstalt. Copyright 1955 by the Estate of Paul Celan.

Published by Princeton University Press
41 William Street, Princeton, New Jersey 08540
99 Banbury Road, Oxford OX2 6JX
press.princeton.edu

GPSR Authorized Representative: Easy Access System Europe - Mustamäe tee 50, 10621 Tallinn, Estonia, gpsr.requests@easproject.com

All Rights Reserved

ISBN 9780691280448
ISBN (pbk) 9780691280462
ISBN (e-book) 9780691288086
ISBN (web PDF) 9780691280479

Library of Congress Control Number: 2025940904

British Library Cataloging-in-Publication Data is available

Editorial: Anne Savarese and Emma Wagh
Production Editorial: Theresa Liu
Text and Jacket / Cover Design: Drohan DiSanto
Production: Lauren Reese
Publicity: William Pagdatoon
Copyeditor: Jodi Beder

Cover images: Courtesy of Brenda Hillman and Unsplash

The Lockert Library of Poetry in Translation is supported by a bequest from Charles Lacy Lockert (1888–1974)

10 9 8 7 6 5 4 3 2 1

CONTENTS

A BRIEF NOTE ON THE AUTHOR AND THE TRANSLATION

There's always a pivot, a "but" or "though" that disturbs the metaphysics of Jeannette L. Clariond's poems. Her books are full of world and yet that world can sometimes seem like a painting, real and not *really* real. Paradox twitches in the heart of her work. What Jeannette writes in regard to the "ocean's dark water" might as well describe the frequent speaker of her poems who so often "gives of herself / what she does not have."

Jeannette L. Clariond is a signal and multifaceted literary nova whose contributions to poetry, translation, and cultural investigation have left an indelible mark on the literary landscape of Mexico. Born in 1949 into a generation that came of age marked by the 1968 Tlatelolco massacre of protesting college students, Jeannette has fashioned a rich and varied body of work that includes—drawing from just the books included in this selection—childhood memoir; one-sentence poetic sequences influenced by paleontology and archeology; outrage with the pandemic of femicides; ancient Mexico; the northern desert border; reflections on art, myth, reincarnation, and existential abandonment. Much of this work has been subtly shaped by her Lebanese origins and her formative years in Chihuahua.

For a Mexican writer, the consequences of growing up in Chihuahua can't be overemphasized. "Chilangos," Jeannette once told me, referring colloquially to the natives of Mexico City, "still think they are the navel of the world. For the chilango, there is only Mexico City, and if you don't live there, artistically speaking, you don't exist." So how did Jeannette's family come to find themselves in the northern state of Chihuahua, noted as much for its cosmopolitan culture as for its vast desert, rugged mountains, and one of the largest canyons in the world, Las Barrancas del Cobre?

In 1902, suffering economic stress and repression inflicted by the Ottoman Empire in the Middle East, many Lebanese emigrated abroad. Jeannette's Lebanese grandmother, then nine years old, was sent with her older brothers on a ship from Beirut to Veracruz, Mexico. That was the first exile. The young girl, tasked with the responsibility of "making a home" for her older brothers in Mexico, married at the age of fourteen a thirty-two-year-old Lebanese immigrant. Soon enough, she had seven children of her own. In a second exile, the family was forced to flee to El Paso after Pancho Villa, during the Mexican Revolution (1910–20), began expropriating land and taking reprisals against Lebanese immigrants.

In El Paso, Jeannette's mother-to-be, Olga, learned English at a Catholic primary school. The family took their religion very seriously. But in the wake of a conflict between Jeannette's grandfather and his brothers, Olga—just an adolescent—was whisked back across the border to Chihuahua, where her father still owned a piece of land. Thus, the third exile. And so Jeannette was born—or "given to the light" as the Mexicans say—in Chihuahua. Jeannette remembers that when she came home from school in those days, her mother, bilingual and well educated, would greet Jeannette at the kitchen door by reciting Hamlet's soliloquy or Kipling's famous poem "If—."

The accretion of these three exiles—"abandonments" Jeannette calls them—came to form a kind of dark pearl of insecurity within the budding poet. In Chihuahua, the vast landscape only exacerbated her anxiousness and sense of isolation. Her mother became increasingly strict and remote. As Jeannette read to keep herself company and as she began to hone her poetic instincts, she developed a signature gnomic syntax, one that often leaps over what Ezra Pound would call the "bookkeeping" words, those familiar articles and coordinating conjunctions that may not be strictly necessary to the meaning. We see this, of course, in her one-line poems from *Ammonites*. But the syntax of the longer poems frequently exhibits a similar elliptical concision. For instance, in "Cicatriz [Scar]," Jeannette writes:

> Teñida de luna, la madre: mundo inventado para aliviar
> lo que aún no es.

Literally,

> Moon-tinted, the mother: world invented to relieve
> what is not yet / what does not yet exist.

Such metonymic compaction can be problematic for the English-language reader—not to mention the translator. We might question the relation in that sentence between "mother" and "world." Is "world" being used as an appositive for "mother"? Possessive determiners are handled differently in Spanish than in English. One doesn't say "My hand hurts"; one says, "*the* hand hurts." So the English reader might wonder if "the mother" is the speaker's ("*my*") mother or perhaps just an endearing renaming of "world" as in the Quechua term "Pachamama," *world-mother*. We might also wonder if allusions to moon and world suggest metaphorical bodies, or maybe persons in orbit around each other. And what does the Heideggerian-sounding "what is not yet" imply?

The appearance of "the mother" in other poems, and the context before and after these lines, suggest to us that after suffering the trauma of having her heel pierced by a strand of barbed wire, the speaker—presumably the young Jeannette talking to herself—thinks of her mother, who notably is not there to comfort her. In place of her absent, self-absorbed mother, the injured child has to construct an imaginary world in which she *is* loved and cared for. In my translation, I try to maintain the concision of the syntax in Spanish, while allowing for just a little readerly guidance:

Moonstruck, my mother: a world needed to be invented
to allay what wouldn't come to be.

Fortunately, because Jeannette not only speaks English, but translates poetry from English into Spanish, I was able to discuss my translations with her. On a few occasions, following our discussions, she adjusted a poem to match the translation. Consequently, the Spanish poems in this selection aren't always precisely the same as when they were originally published.

I chose poems that had never been translated before, and I made my selections from seven of Jeannette's many books to give the reader an indication of her range. Between sections of longer poems, I inserted chapters of one-line sequences from her book *Ammonites*. I imagine that these might not only work as the rhythmical analogues of palette cleansers, changing the pace and mode of the reading, but also allow the reader to re-encounter themes from the sections of longer poems in aphoristic counterpoint.

Among her numerous accolades, Jeannette L. Clariond received the 2021 Juan Felipe Herrera Best Poetry Book Award for *The Goddesses of Water* and the 2022 Pilar Fernández Labrador Award for *Cuerpo de mi sangre / Body of My Blood*. She was also awarded the prestigious Gonzalo Rojas National Poetry Prize for her collection *Todo antes de la noche / All Before the Night*. As a translator, she has undertaken the formidable task of rendering the complete works of renowned authors such as Elizabeth Bishop, Charles Wright, and Primo Levi. Her dedication to translating Italian poet Alda Merini's works earned her recognition from the Alda Merini House Museum in Milan, commemorating Jeannette's twenty-five years of uninterrupted work in translation.

Somehow, along with all this work as a writer and translator, Jeannette has also invented the time to found and run Vaso Roto, an exceptional Spanish-language literary press which serves as a conduit for voices from Mexico, Spain, the United States, France, Italy, Austria, the Arab world, and beyond. Not incidentally, she established Mexico's first annual Braille Poetry Contest.

As an author, Jeannette says that she tries to incorporate multiple voicings from other languages and traditions into her own writing. In consequence, her poems—which she has called "anecdotes endowed with interiority"—employ stylistic variations and shifting tones even while similar concerns recur.

Many of her poems are characterized by their painterly nature and their intense sensuality. Others are so syntactically condensed as to be enigmatic. I take seriously Jeannette's assertion that our charge as both poets and translators is to "translate the spirit of the world, our first and essential task." The spirit of the world and the spirit of the word. Occasionally, my translations diverge from the literal (as if there were such a thing as a literal translation) in order for me to reveal, as best I can, the charge of language carrying a resonance of such density and richness that any word-for-word translation might come across as impenetrable or feel as though it had been handcuffed on its slow, miraculous walk across the bridge of sighs into English.

If, as Ezra Pound noted, "only emotion endures," then Clariond's poems are built to last. For all their psychological acuity and linguistic attentiveness, you'll find that you feel your way through her poems as much as you read them.

Even Time Bleeds

Post canto

Mi cuerpo cae en el agua.

Mi cuerpo ha sido violado

mis restos arrojados a la ciénaga.

Yazgo en el fondo del lodazal.

Permaneceré en el fango

soles, lunas oscuras profundidades, amén.

¿Dónde el verdugo? ¿dónde está él?

La tinta se seca cuando quiero escribir la estela

de rostros lacerados disolviéndose en la sal: los miro

me miran. Cada cuerpo

forma un racimo de humillaciones sobre el limo.

¿Dónde la infinita soledad que suavice los pliegues
    de sus pies?

Post Canto

So my body sinks into the water.

My body raped, its limbs lopped,

slopped into a swamp.

To lie in muck at the bottom

anchored there in the murk

while suns and moons pass over for ever and ever, amen.

And the executioner? where is he?

The ink clots when I try to write of that wake

of lacerated faces dissolving in the swamp: I stare

at them. They stare back. Body after body,

bouquets of excruciations nestling into the clay.

What infinite loneliness begins to soften the creases in
    their feet?

Las piernas de estos cuerpos desmembrados con sus
estigmas y su humillación.

Qué más puede escribirse de estos gritos, asfixias

cuyos ecos se escuchan bajo el agua en donde yazgo

yo también.

Yacemos en la entraña del lodazal.

¿Cómo nombrar el espanto que desgarró el cuerpo de estas
mujeres?

¿Qué decir de los mordiscos sangrando en sus pechos?

¿Qué, además de las lilas ultrajadas, permanece en el camino
de sus huellas?

No hay tumbas. No hay huesos. Ni siquiera ceniza.

Por la mañana el ave canta desde la alambrada

de donde cuelgan las ropas manchadas de tres niñas
desnudas.

¿Quién cubrirá sus cuerpos?

Han regresado al vientre, cabezas adheridas a sus vientres,
sus ojos vendados.

The legs of these dismembered corpses with their stigmata
and shame.

And what could ever be written of the screams and choking

that still echo faintly beneath the water

where I find myself as well.

In the belly of the muck.

How to speak of the terror that tore each of them apart?

Of the bleeding bite marks on their breasts?

What, besides outraged lilacs, remains along the paths of
their footsteps?

There are no graves. No bones. Not even ash.

In the morning, a bird sings from a barbed wire fence

from which hang the bloodied clothes of three naked girls.

Who will cover them?

They are fetal again, their heads tucked toward their
tummies, their eyes blindfolded.

Sueño sus caras como el preámbulo de una desesperanza
  sin fin.

Las horas se acaban sin que pueda dar forma a mi dolor.

El tiempo también sangra.

I dream their faces as the preamble to an endless despair.

The hours expire and still the words remain unformed.

Even time bleeds.

★

Qué intolerable el mundo si no pudiera ser pensado.

★

La poesía es destierro, al origen.

★

Más importante que la creación, la asunción de lo creado.

★

Era el peregrinar su morado, su linterna.

★

El ritmo pausado de la luz moviliza la raíz.

★

El hallazgo, esa invención de lo vivido.

★

Aunque tarde, la palabra encuentra su destino.

★

La sombra, sin su límite, ardería.

★

Por empatía, colocar el tiesto en sano sitio.

★

Intolerable the world if it could not be thought.

★

Poetry is exile, to the origin.

★

More important than creation, the coming to terms
    with creation.

★

Pilgrimage as lived place, its lantern.

★

The slow rhythms of light mobilize the root.

★

Discovery, the invention of the lived.

★

Even late, the word determines the dole.

★

A shadow, minus its limits, would burn off.

★

Out of empathy, placing the pot in a more scenic spot.

★

En la tiniebla, presiente el fulgor del astro.

★

A la orilla somos llevados por la llaga.

★

Al escuchar el límite, reconocerse en él.

★

Logré hacer de tu ausencia mi morada

★

In absolute darkness, she still feels the star's blaze.

★

It's the wound that ferries us to shore.

★

Listening to the limit, then recognizing yourself in it.

★

I succeeded in making your absence my residence.

Desamparo

No, no fue el invierno con su espada de hielo
ni sus brazos cansados.
No fue la lluvia obstinada inundando las cosechas,
tampoco las pardelas en el risco.
Ni siquiera la espesura de las nubes sorbiendo los aleros.
No.
Soy yo con mi acostumbrada ausencia
quien del nido se aleja en la tempestad.

Homelessness

No, it wasn't the winter with an ice sword
held up in its weary arm.
It wasn't the stubborn rain flooding the crops
or the shearwaters at the ridge.
It wasn't even those thick clouds sipping at the eaves.
No.
It was me, me with my habitual absence,
abandoning the nest in the storm.

Pasaje

En un trazo
perfectamente delineado
el horizonte;
en gris
la figura de un hombre
se esfuma entre rojas
y amarillas pinceladas,
luego vuelve más densa y profunda.
La realidad es algo que no acontece;
vivir, sólo un
árbol
de oscura claridad.

Passage

A perfectly delineated
line, the horizon;
grayish,
the figure of a man
vanishes until red
and yellow brushstrokes
give him depth and density.
Reality is something that doesn't
happen; living is something
else: the dark
clarity
of a solitary tree.

Tu rostro por velas alumbrado,
la bruma de tus labios
y el casi transparente cuerpo
al fondo
de raíces desgarradas.
Un último perfume
junto al árbol.
Por la mañana
el viento repite su viaje.
Arde en mí tu ausencia.

Your face lit by candlelight,
the mist of your lips,
and your almost transparent body
down there in that pit
of torn roots.
A trace of your scent
lingers near the tree.
Come morning,
the wind will take up its wandering.
Your absence burns through me.

Mirando lo mirado

Sobre el muro el reflejo.
        Nada es lo mirado,
tampoco lo real es guía de salvación.

El resplandor de dorada fronda
        —todo follaje—
es inicio, pues al caer el sol y la oscuridad
se inscribe sobre las plantas, algo enciende su centro.

La raíz entrega su fronda para hacernos
retroceder hacia el silencio de los nardos
y que el deseo, sangre fresca, abreve en otra nervadura
—espejo del espejo en la simiente—.

Árbol visto en su perfección. Álamo
y sangre. Álamo,
sangre.

El camino de los astros se adelanta al alba,
y desde la tierra crece el vacío.

Un último día la flor vertical, esa vastedad
de cielo que nos mira
mientras lo miramos y hace confluir
        —un solo instante—
las ternuras del agua.

Looking At What's Looked At

On the wall, only reflections.
        Nothing is really there,
nor is the real any guide to salvation.

But the glow of golden leaves
      —all foliage—
is a beginning, for when the sun sets and darkness
writes itself over the plants, something ignites at their core.

A root sends up its frond to convince us
to recede into the silence of fragrant agave,
and to channel the fresh blood of desire into a new vein
—into the mirror of the mirror in the seed—.

At a glance, the tree is flawless. Poplar
and blood. Poplar,
blood.

Each trajectory of the stars is dawnward,
while on earth, our void expands.

One last day, the vertical flower—that vastness
of sky that regards us
while we regard it—will draw together
        in a single instant
all the tendernesses of water.

La inocencia bebe de silvestres violetas
la fugacidad de las estaciones
que cede su paso
a los nevados brotes del peral
antes de que el fruto se desnude.

La realidad se filtra por las precipitaciones
del amor.

Tengo y no tengo la línea en la palma de mi mano,
pez de lenta corriente: su luz huye al roce.

Bajo el agua, las piedras pulen la transparencia.
Bajo el agua, mis pies se alejan de la realidad.

What our innocence sips from wild violets
is the passing of this season
as it gives way
to the emergence of the pear tree's snowy buds
just before its fruit is bared.

The real filters out in the rains
of love.

I have and don't have a telltale line crossing the palm of
     my hand;
like a fish in a slow current: clarity flees at the slightest touch.

Under the water, stones distill the transparency.
Under the water, my feet step away from the real.

Indeleble resplandor

Árbol visto en su perfección. Álamo
y sangre.
Imagen que irradia
lo plata
del envés:
indeleble resplandor
que entre los huecos
de la malla
se filtra.
Al despeñarse sobre el lago
avanza
hacia
ti.
Intacta
permanece
la Palabra.

Indelible Radiance

Perfectly itself, the tree
fixed in your eyes. Poplar
and blood.
An image beaming
its silver undersides:
indelible radiance
fanning out
through little holes
in the tracery.
Plunging into the lake,
the image advances
toward
you.
But what remains
intact
is the Word.

Cicatriz

La luz de la lámpara reabre la cicatriz
y la memoria de otro tiempo
brilla en el empeine enganchado
aquella tarde en la alambrada:

Tú (tú) mirabas el alambre
y esa mirada tuya amarilleaba el horizonte.
La madre, sentada en la sombra,
—un elogio el inicio de su lumbre, ciega parcela su lengua.
El espejo deslloró lágrimas humanas.

Lejos flotaba la casa, el color de la ciudad
cuando la mano esgrafió su mancha en mi piel
y arrancó la púa.

Espuma en lo abierto, la carne entre los dedos
—flores de encina—latía.
La crin del cielo ardió dorada contra el pastizal.
No toques tus ojos, contén la respiración. Calla.

★★★

De aquella carne mía asomó ceniza que deshojó la nieve.
En la farmacia, tras los cubrebocas, hierve la agitación.
Buscas remedio para la cicatriz.

Scar

Falling lamplight seems to reopen the scar
and the memory of another time
gleams where your instep was pierced
one afternoon by a piece of barbed wire:

You (you) stared at the puncture
and as you looked, the horizon yellowed.
Your mother was inside, sitting in the shade,
—only eulogies could spark her fire; what she didn't see
is what kept her quiet. The mirror weeping human tears.

From a distance, your house seemed to float over a colorful city
as your uncle's hand, tracing the gash in your skin,
plucked out the barb.

An ocean breeze, flesh squeezed between fingers
—oak blossoms—it was all pulsing.
The sky's mane flared gold against the grasses.
Don't touch your eyes, hold your breath. Shush now.

★★★

My flesh went ashen; the snow blew off petal by petal.
In the pharmacy, behind face masks, agitation boiled over.
You, seeking some curative for the scar.

Tendrías que haberte quedado en casa. Allí, una violeta.
Teñida de luna, la madre: mundo inventado para aliviar
lo que aún no es.

★ ★ ★

Soñabas cuerpos amortajados en sábanas azules
a la intemperie. Mujeres prendiendo fuego a los cuerpos,
mirando en lo alto los desbocados
        caballos del templo.

★ ★ ★

El mundo es una lengua extendida a lo largo de la calle.

★ ★ ★

He visto nubes de éter elevar sus llantos
hacia un cerrado paraíso. Teníamos silencio, mas canto
        queríamos
de arcilla renacido, ginestas abiertas al estallido del mar.

Clodia, ¿no fue acaso tu belleza lo que dejó a Catulo
        debatiéndose
                entre odio y amor?
Mira ahora mis pies: ¿puedes ver la cicatriz?
El conflicto no está en las plantas que te sostienen.
Amor siempre suma amor. El amor tiene su asiento en la
        palabra.

Madre, mis labios sellaron el papiro sobre tus ojos,
                hace ya tiempo muertos.

You should have stayed home. Potted like a violet.
Moonstruck, my mother: a world needed to be invented
to allay what wouldn't come to be.

★ ★ ★

You dreamed of bodies shrouded in blue sheets
lying out in the open. Of women setting fire to corpses,
looking up to take in the rampaging
                    temple horses.

★ ★ ★

The world is a huge tongue unfurling itself down the street.

★ ★ ★

I've seen ethereal clouds lifting their supplications
toward a shuttered paradise. We were granted silence, but
     what we wanted was to sing of freshly dug clay, of Spanish
     broom in blossom by the bursting sea.

Clodia, wasn't it your beauty that left Catullus wishy-washy
                    about hate and love?
Look at my feet now: can you see the scars?
The conflict isn't about what it is we stand on.
Love always adds to love. Love, which makes its home in the
     word.

Mother, my lips sealed the papyrus over your eyes, your eyes
                    so long ago extinguished.

Cielo de sombras

Nacidos de la mano de Dios, los pájaros oscurecieron el cielo.
Habituados a la luz, olvidamos cómo leer las sombras.
Puliremos
la palabra
como hemos pulido la escudilla de plata.
Ignoramos
la ciencia que guarda toda oscuridad,
la que anima al tacto,
y así podamos comprender
la soledad del olmo en la ribera.

Olvidamos los nombres de la tierra por pretender ser mar.

Una monotonía de mentiras
lacra la cera en labios de las urnas.
¿En dónde estabas tú, oh rosa, dónde?, ¿por qué
en mis ojos te extinguías?
Samara, mi espíritu guardián, me dejas
sólo este espejo de follaje.
Yo también olvido los nombres.

Soy arena dispersa; ansié la demasiada luz.

Sky of Shadows

Loosed from the Lord's hand, birds darken the sky.
Habituated to light, we forget how to read shadows.
We'll come to polish
the word
as we've polished a silver bowl.
We brush aside
the science, laded with darkness,
which brings feeling to our touch,
while we try to understand
the loneliness of the elm on the riverbank.

We're like a sea that lost track of the land.

A monotony of lies
seals the wax over the lips of urns.
Where were you, o rose, where? Why
did you flicker out in my eyes?
Samara,[1] my guardian spirit, you left me
just this mirror reflecting leaves.
I too forgot the names.

I'm scattered sand; I craved too much light.

Corylus avellana

La palabra nace de semilla indehiscente.
Flor de abismo, su herida marca a quien la toca;
deja un brillo extraño en los ojos
y te hunde en la profundidad de la tinta;
su aroma de pronto concentra
tu esencia en qué pedacería de espejos
que te regresa a aquellas
conversaciones en el cuarto de atrás o voces que llevas dentro.
La palabra es la estrella que predice tu destino,
esa inevitable simulación, una alegría
que se imprime en tu rostro temporariamente y que,
al salir de casa, como sales del sueño al alba,
te regresa a una cierta normalidad
que no acaba de ajustarse.
Mis palabras nunca acaban de ajustarse.
Miente el río en que nos miramos: la luz
de la palabra es siempre una forma de ausencia:
un resplandor flotando más allá del horizonte.

Corylus avellana

The word is born from an indehiscent seed.
Like an abyssal flower, it wounds all who touch it;
it leaves a strange gleam in your eyes
and immerses you in inky depths;
its scent suddenly concentrates
your essence into some shards of mirror
that return you to those
backroom conversations, voices carried inside you.
The word's a star foretelling your destiny,
that inevitable simulation, a gladness
briefly imprinted on your face,
but when you wake from dream and leave home,
you feel restored to some kind of normalcy
that never quite fits.
My words never quite fit.
The river in which we see ourselves tells a lie: the light
of the word will forever remain a form of absence:
a radiance flowing past the edge of sight.

Del lado de la bruma

Derramada sangre, comencé a escribirte
antes de nacer.
¿Cómo es tu rostro ahora?
Te oigo llorar en mis sueños,
oh, pálida Rosa de la Paz, te oigo llorar.
Llevas dentro un sol que asoma a la deriva.
Pero, tú, ¿conocías la dicha o eras
la imagen de la noche que a todos desconoce?
La voz es una sed de forma.
Para hallarla, he dejado de rodar en el vacío.

El remordimiento, la ira, la culpa–mi madre
es un país alejado del mío, piedad de abismos.
¿Y debo dar voz ahora a mi boca?
No, hubiera preferido escucharla.
Recorrí valles y collados y ciudades
nevadas hasta forzar este silencio en mi garganta.
Soñaba a mi madre flotar en aguas someras,
envuelta en algas,
dentro de un sarcófago marfil.
Y su voz me gritaba, y con una mano yo cubría
mi boca y con la otra,
mis ojos, y yo le juraba
que no era yo quien había traicionado su secreto,
ese secreto que sólo yo
supe entrever.

Off in the Mist

With leaked blood, I began to write you
even before my birth.
What does your face look like now?
I hear you weeping in my dreams,
oh, pale Peace Rose, I hear you groan.
Inside yourself, you lug the unanchored sun.
But tell me, did you ever find bliss or did you just turn
into some image of night no one can recognize?
Any voice is a thirst for form.
I no longer stumble through the void to find mine.

Remorse, rage, guilt—my mother
is a country remote from me, a mercy in an abyss.
And must I now give voice to my own mouth?
No, I would have preferred to listen to hers.
I wandered valleys and hills and snowy
cities while this silence was jammed down my throat.
I dreamed my mother was floating in shallow water,
swathed in seaweed,
inside an ivory sarcophagus.
And her voice came at me like a squall. And with one hand
I covered my mouth and with the other,
my eyes, and I swore to her
that it wasn't me who gave up her secret,
the secret that only I
had discerned.

Cuando toqué la orilla de la espuma,
su sangre me introdujo mar adentro.

Just when I set foot on the foaming shore,
her blood whooshed me out to sea.

Écfrasis

Cuando la incisión abra la herida, ¿quién pondrá sobre
  tu rostro
los cálices embebidos en sangre, quién derramará
el púrpura por donde pases camino al alba?

Alguien será portador de los cuerpos. Me asomaré por la
  ventana
y el sollozo reflejará el vaho
como recuerdo en medio de los tulipanes.

Nadie crece inmune a la desgracia, lo sé.
Ni el genio, ni el bosque, ni Dios.
¿Añorabas desde tu lecho la densa niebla en los Cárpatos?
Antschel, déjame conocerte, duerme en lo más dormido de
  mi corazon.
Duerme. Tu mano no enturbiará mi tinta, duerme.
No seque el humo el alba de tu rosa—esa rosa
      que no es de nadie.

Puedo sentir tu anhelo de presencia.

Lo que sale de las bocas de los otros
semeja largos filamentos
de esa rosa cercada por las llamas.

Ekphrasis

When the incision reopens the wound, who will set beside
    your face
the blood-soaked chalices, who will cloak with imperial purple
the casket in which I see you on your way to the next dawn?

Someone will haul the bodies. I'll lean from the window
and my sobbing will ricochet through the mist
like some memento lost in a cluster of tulips.

No one grows immune to misfortune, I know.
Not genius, not the forest, not even God.
From your bed, were you dreaming of that heavy
    Carpathian fog?
Antschel,[2] let me know you, sleep now in the quietest
    chamber of my being.
Sleep. Your hand can't smudge my ink, so sleep.
And I'll keep the smoke from blurring the dawn of your
    rose—that rose
        which is no one's.

I can feel your yearning for presence.

What escapes the mouths of others
looks to me like long filaments
radiating from a flame-encircled rose.

Traducirte, vivir más cerca de la roca.

Yo también voy cavando la fosa. Con la palabra, sigo
cavando en el polvo de los huesos,
ese espacio ausente y sus labios de ceniza.

—Muy pronto también yo me habré ido.
Duerme.
En cada vocablo se entreabre el alma de las cosas.

Translating you, I live ever closer to the fissure.

And I too go on digging the pit. Taking up the word, I dig
and keep digging down through the dust of bones,
to an absent space lipped with ash.

—Soon enough, I too will be gone.
Sleep.
With each vocable, the soul of things comes clearer.

Anselm Kiefer me escucha

Dice verdad quien dice sombra.

—PAUL CELAN

Una brizna de cobrizo marfil, su cuerpo sepulto en Thiais.
Flores trágicas derraman su ceniza sobre
la sorda reminiscencia del musgo.
Tus libros recogen las páginas apiladas en el Sena de Genet,
la correspondencia del astro con el azul-nevado del campo
desde donde te miro elevarte en esquirlas de humo.
Los sarcófagos tiñen el fango, charcas rojas velan los cuerpos
y la negra leche del alba te conduce hacia el fin.
En el vasto espacio, el tallo del tulipán alza su fuego.
Mechones, muros de arcilla, árboles de purpúreos troncos
caen en un orden extraño. El cáliz de la amapola enciende
el prodigio del sueño de Zulamith. Y tú, detrás del agujero
en el lienzo:
ásperas, rugosas, espesas capas los campos de girasoles en
Barjac
y, más abajo, la serpiente.
La máquina no se ha detenido.
Zulamith bebe la negra leche, cava hasta desenterrar el
temblor
de la arboleda. Araña muy dentro del corazón el odio

Anselm Kiefer Hears Me Out

Speaks true who speaks shadow.
—PAUL CELAN

A blade of copper-colored ivory, his body buried in Thiais.
Tragically, flowers drop their ash over
some vague reminiscence of moss.
Your books bind together all those pages stacked up by
    Genet's Seine,
the correspondence of a star and the snowy-blue countryside
from where I watch you rising on wisps of smoke.
The sarcophagi cast shadows into the mud, red pools
    overlie bodies
while the black milk of dawn leads you to the finish.
In vast space, the stem of a white tulip hoists its flame.
Tufts, walls of clay, trees with purple trunks
assemble in a strange order. The poppy's calyx ignites
the wonder of Shulamit's dream. And you, behind that hole
    in the canvas:
taking in the stony, thickly carpeted fields of sunflowers
    in Barjac
and below the flowers' stems, the viper.
The machine hasn't stopped.
Shulamit drinks the black milk, digs down to disinter
    the tremor
below the grove. She claws open the rage in her breast

los surtidores de ceniza. Pero ahora
has desanudado la azulina cabellera de la amada.
Tu boca entre sierpes; tu lienzo nos concede
la confidencia de la roca transida de estrellas, el fragor
  calcinado del mar.
Contra el fondo bronce, tu cascada de oro, Margarethe,
puede aún nos rescatarnos
mientras sigamos sostenidos de la sirga.

releasing fountains of ash. But now
you've untied your beloved's bluish hair.
Your mouth, encircled by snakes; your canvas offers us
the conviction of a rock riddled with stars, the dessicated
  clamor of the sea.
Against all that bronze background, your golden waterfall,
  Margarete,
might yet rescue us
as long as we cling for our lives to the rope.

Mujer de arena

En la playa el cuerpo de una mujer
semeja un continente.
En su rostro toda la vida de un sueño.
Se encamina hacia las peñas, se disipa
sin mirar hacia atrás.
No intentó detenerse en la curva,
como si ningún remordimiento estremeciese su alma.
De pronto era nube
que borraba toda imagen o recuerdo
para luego desvanecerse
en las rocas.
El mar la devolvía a la vida,
a su lugar
en lo cristalino
pero yo sentía que en cualquier momento
la perdería para siempre.
Corrí hacia ella,
la estreché ola desnuda,
mis brazos temblaban
irremediablemente,
condenada a la culpa.
Quise retenerla.
No era que se fuera, me inquietaba
el remordimiento.
Aunque su pulso latía, yo sabía que su cuerpo
acabaría abruptamente desleído en la playa.

Woman of Sand

On the beach, a woman's body
resembles a continent.
She carries in her face a dream life.
Approaching the sea stacks, she starts to dissolve
without looking back.
But she doesn't hesitate at the wave's curl.
It's as though no remorse were shaking her soul.
And so she explodes into a spray
that erases every image or memory
as it hisses out
against the rocks.
It was the sea that brought her back to life,
to her place
in the crystalline,
but I knew that at any moment
I might lose her forever.
I raced toward her,
and embraced the naked wave,
my arms trembling
helplessly
with guilt. How
I wanted to hold her back.
It wasn't so much her leaving, but my remorse
that unsettled me.
For though I felt her pulse beating, I knew her body
would collapse and evanesce on the beach.

★

Cada pérdida pone un abismo en el ojo y la cuerda para salir de él.

★

Es desde el puente que reconoces la turbulencia.

★

Dilatado fuego, la noche en que se ama.

★

La agitación es el sosiego de la abeja.

★

Se abre la flor al vacío de su entrega.

★

Nostalgia del viaje hacia la voz perdida.

★

¿Quién acaricia tus manos que tan bien acarician?

★

El instante no descansa en su búsqueda de cercanía.

★

El enigma de surcar lado a lado la sed.

★

With each loss, an abyss in the eye and the rope to climb
    out of it.

★

It's from the bridge that you recognize the turbulence.

★

A swelling flame, the night of love.

★

Agitation is the bee's tranquility.

★

The flower opens into the emptiness of its arrival.

★

The nostalgic journey for the lost voice.

★

Who caresses your hands which are so talented at caressing?

★

An instant never rests in its search for nearness.

★

The enigma of plowing forward side by side with your thirst.

★

La palabra necesitada de consuelo es signo de su fuego
  naciendo.

★

Seguir la huella de la luz nacida dentro.

★

Sentí tu corriente entrar al mar, amé su nocturna tibieza.

★

Dulce en el ocaso el envero de la vid.

★

En la embriaguez, ¿quién recuerda las semillas de la uva?

★

Vaga por la lengua ese vocablo que quisimos destruir.

★

En el viento escuché la flor que calla en el poema.

★

Sosiegan al viento las hojas de los álamos.

★

La plena desnudez es cielo seguro.

★

In its need for consolation, a word's first fire is lit.

★

To follow the trace of a light born inside you.

★

I felt your current run to the sea, I loved its night-warmth.

★

So sweet at twilight, the vine's ripening.

★

Drunk, who remembers the seeds of the grape?

★

The word we would extirpate still wanders through the
language.

★

In wind I heard the flower that went silent in the poem.

★

It's the leaves of the poplar that calm the wind.

★

Nakedness is safe haven.

★

En la melancolía, entregarse el poema.

★

El espejo me mira sin saber a quién mira.

★

No modificar la esencia del río, sólo su curso.

★

Quise escapar de la muchedumbre, las risas, mis vacíos.

★

In melancholy, the poem gives itself up.

★

The mirror observes me not knowing who it observes.

★

Not to change the river's nature, but only to alter its course.

★

I longed to escape the crowds, the laughter, my emptiness.

El viento
desmoronaba el barro,
vértigo, dolor era ese viento
en su descenso:
        el encuentro
        con la primera voz:
la muerte.

        El muro de raíz sedienta
rasga cielos
de aquella hora.

De nuevo
brotarán salmos
palabras destejiendo
sobre el espejo.

Wind
pulverized the mud,
vertigo, a wind which was pure
pain subsiding:
      an encounter
      with the first voice:
death's voice.

      At this very hour,
an upturned bank of thirsting roots
flails at the sky.

Surely
palms will flourish again
but for now, my words go to pieces
in the mirror.

Apenas el agua circundó la tierra
en su centro
se abrieron cavidades:
el viento devoró las copas de los cedros,
los nidos, el rostro de aquella voz.

Creer, crear la oración
que nombre su presencia,
el misterio
de su alma desprendida.

When water encircled the earth's
waist,
cavities opened:
wind swallowed the tips of cedars,
the nests, and the face behind your voice.

How to believe, to beget the prayer
that might call forth your presence,
the mystery
of your severed soul.

Todo era tiniebla
(de raíz),
arteria
dilatada
cuando el viento
derrumbó la cúpula.

En vano
la tierra hunde
su perpetuo nacer.

All was darkness
(root-dark),
an artery
dilated
as wind
upended the cupola.

To no avail,
the land buries
what it perpetually gives birth to.

Cielo esta boca, hojas
la orilla,
el río congelado
y la tierra del recuerdo
evaporando
su fragmento de piel.

Mi ser,
mi ser errante,
mi ser,
miseria entrando,
mi ser
          silueta.

Lo que no fui, siendo
afina su sombra.

Ceguera: ahí estarás.

Sky, a mouth; some leaves,
the shore;
a frozen river
and the land of memory
sloughs off
its little scrap of skin.

My being,
my errant being,
my being,
with pain rushing in,
the fractured silhouette
        of my being.

What I am only sharpens
the shadow of what I was not.

Blindness: I've found you.

Hay regiones que son sílabas de sombras.

There are zones that are no more than the syllables of
shadows.

Desde lo hondo
al viento
la dispersa ruina.

Morir, morir dentro
del árbol
al aire y lumbre
florecido.

Hija del hambre,
tus pasos segará
la pétrea luna.

From the abyss
to the wind,
the ruin spreads.

To die, to die inside
the tree
holding its blossoms out
to air and fire.

Hunger's daughter,
look how your approach cuts loose
the stony moon.

Voces, voces distantes,
espejos,
palabras piedra:
Todo antes de la noche.

Voices, far off voices,
mirrors,
words of stone:
They all assemble before the night.

Descarnada belleza,
de ti
busco salvarme.

Fleshless beauty,
it's from you
I long to save myself.

Hay una luz
en su aliento
de árbol,
pájaros
de aquella tarde
en fuego revestida
sobre los huertos.
Luz
el aliento del árbol.
Pájaros,
hombres,
y el bosque:
ascienden juntos
en un carro de fuego.

There's a light
inside the
trees' breath,
birds
on an afternoon
sheathed in fire
that smothers the orchards.
Light,
the breathing trees.
Birds,
men,
and forest:
they soar upward together
in a chariot of fire.

Amar la luz
de aquella nube de ceniza,
los once túneles,
las huellas de las bestias,
caminos que entre las humaredas
caen del cielo.

Tierra dispersa de semilla,
guarda la salvación,
el silencio en la piedra,
la mirada del río en su sollozo.

Tierra dispersa de ceniza,
guarda la salvación,
ama la luz de aquella nube,
amar los límites,
        el alba en llamas.

To love the light
falling from a cloud of ash,
the eleven tunnels,
the tracks of animals,
roads that, cloaked in smoke,
unroll from the sky.

Dirt scattered with seed,
hope for life to come,
silence at the stone's heart,
and the glimpse of a sobbing river.

Dirt sprinkled with ashes,
hope for life to come,
love the cloud-light,
love the limits,
                this flaming dawn.

Bajo el manto de fuego
la luz emerge
de su cuerpo
—mundo, hora, humanidad–
ya casi muertos
a la espera del comienzo.

Below a mantle of fire
light emanates
from the body
—world, time, humankind—
we're nearly dead
as we hold on for the beginning.

Van los hombres y las cosas
hacia la estancia primera.
La travesía es la voz.
Del monzón de arenas
emerge lo olvidado,
el polvo se levanta
en pequeños círculos.
Van a la entrada
del silencio.
A lo largo
la quietud,
la sagrada quietud
del sueño que los sueña.

Men and things head off
toward their first way station.
Their journey is their voice.
From the monsoon of sands
what has been forgotten emerges,
dust rises
in tiny whirlwinds.
They press themselves to the entrance
of silence.
And all along
stillness,
that sacred stillness
of the dream which dreams them all.

Cures tu ceguera
en las aguas de Lagash.
Tu corazón no es nada
sino la noche
agitando su sueño.

Buscas perdón
y la palabra *río*
abre hasta el fondo la voz:

Aún escucho su inmensidad.

May you cure your blindness
in the waters of Lagash.
Your heart is nothing
but the night
stirring its dream.

When you seek forgiveness,
the word *river*
pours into the channel of your voice.

Even now I hear its immensity.

En tus ojos
la historia desgarrada,
las luchas, los animales fieros.
Busco salvarte:
Aj ibur shapu, No persevere el enemigo oculto,
no sea su sangre en tu vasija.
Rostro sin velo,
cuanto has temido
cada tarde
regresa
mientras das sorbos en la *demitasse.*

In your eyes,
a torn history of
exertions, savage animals.
If I could, I'd save you:
Aj-ibur-shapu:[3] May the invisible enemy not prevail,
may his blood never pass into your cup.
With your face unveiled,
all the fear you've held in
surges back
each evening
as you sip your demitasse.

Una flecha en el barro con la inscripción *ti*
alumbra ("*enliti*" es palabra) a los elegidos
bajo el reinado del león.
Los dioses resguardan Tell Brak
cuando el oscuro jadeo del viento.

Mi cuerpo es ramas
y el cielo
    insostenibles portones borrosos.

An arrow in the mud bearing the inscription *ti*
enlightens ("*enliti*" is the word) those chosen
under the reign of the lion.
The gods guard Tell Brak
when the dark wind begins panting.

My body is all branches
and the sky,
       a swirling, indefensible gate.

Penumbra en el alabastro,
montes de limo bajo las frondas,
maderos de cedro
y tú,
espejeante entre las dunas.

Ciega a tu destino
de la mano vas
hacia el abismo del conocimiento.

Shadowfall on alabaster,
hills of silt beneath the fronds,
cedar beams—
and you,
a shimmer among the dunes.

Oblivious to what's to come,
with your one hand gripping the other, you head off
into the chasm of knowing.

El oro de las nubes se desliza
en la espesura
de tu paso, paquidermo, por Siam.
Piedras preciosas ornan tu cabeza,
accedo al árbol de purpúreas hojas
que me hablan de aquella luna
sobre tu piel. En tu trompa
ramas
recién arrancadas
son cielos de plegaria.

La memoria es presencia,
fruto de lo vivido,
en equilibrio avanza, vidente,
hacia el verdor.

Cloud-gold sifts
down into the thickets
of your tramping through Siam.
Gemstones on your elephantine head.
I've come to a tree with purple leaves
redolent somehow
of the moon's light
on your thick, gray skin. You,
who raise freshly torn branches
toward the sky like prayers.

Memory itself is presence,
the very fruit of what's been lived,
pressing forward—balanced, clairvoyant—
further into the green world.

Más allá de tu piel, más
hondo que tus huesos,
el dolor, el dolor.

Boca de este canto,
espejo eres.

Beyond your skin, deeper
even than your bones,
the pain, the pain.

This song's open mouth
is your mirror.

★

La estrella se hunde en su extrañeza.

★

Arde desde la raíz la flor.

★

Renace de la rama desnuda el ave que al otoño se ofrenda.

★

Como el libro, nacemos de un mismo vacío. Estamos obligados a ser nuestra propia invención.

★

Impaciencia, ese húmedo leño.

★

Si el sufrimiento no acaricia, no es completo.

★

La forma del fuego se desparrama en sombras.

★

Escribir, dar la cara a la tormenta.

★

The star sinks into its strangeness.

★

From root upward the flower burns.

★

Reborn from the bare branch, the bird gifts itself to autumn.

★

Like a book, we're born from emptiness. Forced to be our
own invention.

★

Impatience, that wet log.

★

If suffering doesn't also caress, it's incomplete.

★

The fire's size is amplified by its shadows.

★

In writing, to turn your face into the storm.

★

Nunca pierdes nada. Estás en la Nada.

★

El poeta devora su propio fuego.

★

Quebradizo es el movimiento de la pluma en la embarcación.

★

La pasión deja rescoldos de ruidoso silencio.

★

Cuántos atardeceres mide un camino.

★

En el dolor, mi madre se convertía en mi hija.

★

Sin pasión por el vacío y la Nada no existe realidad en el poema.

★

Como cascada seca baja la raíz de la magnolia.

★

La ceguera ve en el amor, acrece en el temor.

There's nothing you can lose. You're inside the Nothing.

★

The poet swallows her own fire.

★

Almost trembly, the swing of the boat's boom.

★

Passion leaves behind embers of deafening silence.

★

How many sunsets does a road record?

★

In her despair, my mother became my daughter.

★

Without a passion for emptiness and Nothingness, the poem
    fails to register the real.

★

Like a dry waterfall, the root of the magnolia plunges
    downward.

★

In love blindness sees; in fear it winks out.

★

Algo se olvida al aleteo del colibrí.

★

Antes del viaje, el temor al Viaje.

★

En la elección del camino, deja que decida el camino.

★

Hay palabras cuyo sino es nunca ser pronunciadas.

★

¿Escucha el zumbido el destino de la abeja?

★

Mil sueños desparrama tu vida errante.

★

La ausencia surca los mares de la muerte.

★

Bruscamente la dársena se abrió al mar, y la corriente, súbita, entró en mí.

★

El agua en que me miraba era troceado espejo, sólo miraba mi propia confusión.

★

Glimpsing the hummingbird's wings, something else is
forgotten.

★

Before the journey, fear of Journey.

★

When choosing the right road, wait for the road to decide.

★

There are words whose fate is never to be uttered.

★

Does the buzz hear the bee's fate?

★

A thousand dreams scatter your life outward.

★

It's absence that sails the seas of death.

★

Abruptly, the dock opened to the sea, and the current
suddenly overwhelmed me.

★

The water in which my reflection caught was a broken
mirror; what I glimpsed was my own confusion.

★

No obstante las circunstancias, al mar nada lo perturba; sabe
que siempre será mar.

★

La boca no sabe lo que dice, su verdad es ola que se disuelve
en la ola.

★

En cada vocablo se entreabre, apenas vislumbrada, la gracias
inmarcesible de las cosas.

★

Despite circumstances, nothing disrupts the sea; it knows it
will always be the sea.

★

The mouth can't make out what it speaks, its truth—a wave
dissolves in the wave.

★

Each word begins to open, so liminally: the unfading grace
of things.

Desnuda te esperé

publicado como una cantata
por el Auditorio Nacional de España, 2021

Apenas se oía el polvo,
latía la luz en los intersticios de la veneciana,
y tú esperabas la llegada de la galera.
Flotaba el brillo en el oleaje. Remos a la orilla.
¿Llegó o se fue la embarcación?
Casi todo resplandecía. Casi todo.
¿Por qué el sauce no se reflejó en la alberca?
El ave sí cantó, a pesar del vaticinio,
callado viento de azafrán
habitaría esa noche la pradera.
Eras tú entrando en la habitación, tú atravesando el aire.
Desnuda te esperé. La bañera rebosaba deseo,
el árbol inclinado, la humedad suave
del tacto, los azulejos, la luz
de la cerámica en los cuerpos.
Luego, el reposo de la llama. Ciegos
nos hundimos en el lino,
roces que colman el abandono
cuando al hielo regresan los cisnes.

Naked I Waited for You

published as a cantata
by the National Auditorium of Spain, 2021

The dust was almost audible,
light throbbed through the venetian blind slats,
as you waited for the galley to arrive.
Glitter floated over the waves. Oars on the shore.
But did the boat arrive or depart?
Almost everything glowed. Almost everything.
Where was the willow's reflection in the pool?
A bird went on singing, despite the predictions;
a quiet saffron wind
settled into the meadow's night.
Then it was you entering the room, you passing through
    the air.
Naked, I waited for you. The bathtub brimmed with desire,
the tree leaned toward our window, I recall
the soft dampness of touching, blue tiles, a porcelain
light falling over our bodies.
Then, the flame at rest. Blind,
we sank into the linen, into a friction
that could only complete our abandonment—
as when swans return to the ice.

Mina 1004

Arder, yo vi a mi abuela arder.
Agosto. Chihuahua, 1963. Ella ardió,
su fuera y su dentro, ardió en la calle Mina 1004.
Vi a mi padre envolverla en una sábana, el colchón ardía;
las cortinas, la alfombra, su vestido
ennegrecieron. Todo lo recogió.
«No hagan ruido, su madre está cansada».
Lo vi de luto esa tarde de agosto con su corbata negra.
La recogió. Ceniza y llanto recogió.

El humo de la abuela en el zaguán, las tías
sorbiendo, ásperos, los grumos del café.

Había que borrar lo oscuro que dolía,
disolver la sal, el llanto,
abrazarse y sofocar el temblor del viaje.
Escuchar a Paul Anka y en la falta de pulso
rayar el disco de 45 revoluciones por minuto.

Por instantes vivía, por instantes
todo fue púrpura: la mujer, el
cansancio, las frondas de los álamos. Después
el vidrio, el vidrio en el cedro,
el rostro quemado bajo el humo.

1004 Mina Street

Burning, I saw my grandmother burning.
August. Chihuahua, 1963. She burned,
without and within, burned at 1004 Mina Street.
I watched my father wrap her in a sheet, the mattress on fire;
the curtains, the carpet, her dress
carbonized. He gathered everything up.
"Don't make a sound," he said, "your mother's exhausted."
I saw him in mourning that August afternoon in his black tie.
Ashes and weeping, he gathered it all up.

The smoke of my grandmother's flesh lingered in the hallway
while my aunts went on sipping bitter clots of coffee.

I needed to rub away the stinging darkness,
to rinse out the salt, the weeping,
to be held, and to stifle the tremor of passage.
I listened to Paul Anka, and for want of a heartbeat,
I gouged a scratch across that 45 rpm record.

For brief moments, I lived, for brief moments
everything went purple: the woman who was gone,
the fatigue, the poplar leaves. Afterwards,
through the viewing glass, through the clear plate in her
    cedar casket,
I made out her scorched visage cured with smoke.

Ella, mi madre, también ardió. En lágrimas su sonrisa
  apagada:
«Arréglame el pelo, me dijo, déjame salir
a ver si ya está seca la ropa».

Tuve miedo. De que sus pasos lentos no volvieran, de la tersura
  de la hoja, del sigiloso carcomer,
del reseco peso de la hiedra, ya sin muro, del
florero en la cocina, sin flores. De ese cuarto ciego
  con su muerte tuve miedo.
De mí misma y el filtrarse del viento
que se llevaba el polvo de los sicomoros.

As for my own mother, she burned in a different way. Tears
snuffed out her smile: "Fix my hair," she'd tell me. "Let me
go outside to check if the clothes are dry."

I was terrified. Of the thought that her slow footsteps
        wouldn't return,
of the leaf's suppleness, of a stealthy gnawing inside me,
of the brittle weight of ivy missing its supporting wall,
of the vase in the kitchen minus its flowers. Of that
        blind room with its death, I was terrified.
And of myself and of the divvying wind
that dragged off the dust of the sycamores.

El poeta

1
Polvo
finísimo
que nadie ve.

Vidriosa soledad
que da al cuerpo
lo que no
sabe.

Alma que engendra otra alma.

Dice
mis ojos están rotos.

Clama en el vacío
por la luz
que un día fue paraíso.

Cuando deja de ver,
alumbra.

The Poet

1
There's dust
so fine
no one sees it.

And a glassy loneliness
conveying to the body
what it doesn't
know.

Soul engendering soul.

She says,
My eyes have broken.

Crying into the void
for the light
that once was her paradise.

Then, just when she can see no more,
the light brightens.

2

No acepta que su visión se incline hacia lo grandioso,
como si el vacío
guiara su mano, el color de su tinta.
Su morada semeja las valvas de una ostra,
allí concentra lo disperso
hasta florecer
perla,
nácar que lo regresa siempre a casa.
Suya es la sombra,
una sombra intuitiva,
discontinua.
Está en la luz, filo de ceguera
que asierra el sueño,
pero su voz
persiste
blanca muselina
muy dentro
de la blancura.
Reclama la aridez del vocablo.
Y su dolor
se precipita en silencio.

2

She won't accept that her vision tends toward the grandiose,
as if it were the void
that guides her hand, her handwriting.
Her dwelling resembles the valves of an oyster
where dross condenses
until it blossoms
into pearl,
a nacre she calls home.
The shadow is hers,
an intuitive shadow
intermittent.
She's there in the light, where the blade
of blindness severs dream,
but her interior voice
persists—
faint as white muslin
deep inside
a greater whiteness.
She still insists on the aridity of the word.
And so her pain
precipitates into silence.

3
La textura oculta de la ostra
siega su dicha.

El poeta
se deslíe
en el lago de la palabra
como planeo del ánsar.

Su visión es blanca,
laten sus sienes,
laten con el pulso del río.

Pero ha encontrado el lugar
de su ilegitimidad
donde se mira
de nuevo
luchando
dolidamente
con las cenizas.

3
There is something, she thinks, to value
in the occult texture of the oyster.
The poet
slides
into the lake of the word
like landing geese.
Her vision goes white,
the pulse in her temple beats
with the river's pulse.
But she's reached the place
of her illegitimacy
where she finds herself
once again
wrestling
achingly
with ashes.

4
Muda cadencia, el poeta es relámpago suspendido en la
    encrucijada,
sol que despunta en la azucena, nunca engañado por
    el cristal.
Mancha de ocelote, se derrama sin traspasar su impronta.
Avanza protegido por su segura sombra. Curtida raíz,
su silencio aguarda como limo en el fondo del pozo.
Erosión y aurora, su grito estalla flor de abismo.

4

Mute cadence, the poet flares like lightning at the crossroads,
the sun breaks over a lily, undistracted by the transparence
   of things.
The ocelot's spots spill from the animal and leave no trace.
She moves forward, using her shadow as her shield. A
   weathered root,
her silence on hold, like slime at the bottom of a well.
Erosion and aurora, and then her cry erupts: a flower
   of abyss.

Pavo real

Una leyenda sufí dice que Dios creó el
Espíritu en forma de pavo real.

El ave despliega su propio pasado.
Su luz resiste
en el reflejo del agua.
Viento sobre las lilas,
un paraíso de infinitos ojos contempla
el cobalto iridiscente derramarse
sobre la estela fiel del lago.
Lo que observo, sé que
nunca se repetirá, pues el pavo real,
sólo una vez se revela.
Abre su pecho, transmutar
su belleza en pura geometría. Pienso
en el cristal y los jardines
de la memoria mientras las aves
acompañan el murmullo del río. Esta vez,
me hace sentir
entero su misterio, la grieta, la llamarada.
Sólo existo porque me mira.

Peacock

A Sufi legend says God created the
Spirit in the form of a peacock.

The bird puts his own past on display.
His light sustained
in the reflective water.
Wind over the lilacs,
a paradise of infinite eyes beholds
an iridescent cobalt spilling
onto the lake in faithful array.
What I witness, I already know
will never be repeated, since the peacock
reveals itself like this just once.
His chest swells, transmuting
his beauty into a pure geometry. I think
of stained glass and the garden
of memory while the bird floats by
on the river's murmur. This once,
he lets me feel
all his mystery, the flame, the wound.
I exist because he sees me.

Ayuno

El poeta no quiso ayunar en el Ramadán
ni comer la carne de los sacrificios.
No ahuyentó camellos hacia La Meca
ni se levantó al alba para asistir a la casa de la oración.
Sus actos nobles los convirtió en beber del vino
de Hasim, alzar tiendas en el desierto, bajar sus ojos
en la raíz sacra de los vocablos.

Y cuando su vista alzaba, era
para sentir el aroma del jazmín.
Y ver brillar la mañana.

Fasting

The poet didn't fast during Ramadan
or eat the flesh of sacrifice.
He drove no camels to Mecca.
Didn't rise at dawn to bow in the house of prayer.
He translated the acts of his life
into drinking Hasim's[4] wine, raising tents in the desert,
lowering his eyes to the sacred root of words.

And when he raised his face, it was
only to register the scent of jasmine.
To see the morning glisten.

La huida

¿Qué plasma amoroso me regresará la esperanza de un alba
   sin mancha?
El tiempo de mis arrugas hace temblar el tiempo de mi
   fruición.

No tolero ver más piernas descarnadas
ni estériles brazos de madres sin sus hijos.

Les dejo el mando. Salgo a beber del rubí suave.
Voy a donde despiertan las flores,
adonde el pozo está saciado y la copa colmada de dátiles.

The Escape

What platelet-rich plasma will give me back hope?
This time of my wrinkling makes the time of my
   ripening tremble.

I can't bear to see any more bony legs
or the barren arms of mothers without children.

I leave the command to you. I'm off to drink ruby wine.
I'm called to go where the flowers are waking,
where the well is high and the cup, filled with dates.

Vacío

No, no fuiste amada,
acaso traspasado tu cuerpo.
Temblaron tus labios,
se estremeció tu piel.
Pero no, no fuiste amada.
Ardió solo el árbol
en el centro
de tu vida
y en tu lecho amaste
mirando palidecer la luz
de otra mirada.
El cuerpo, al cabo, vencerá al amor.
Y al sordo rumor de las perlas
vestirás un mismo luto.

Empty

No, no, you were not loved,
though your body may have been pierced.
Your lips trembled,
your skin quivered.
But no, you were not loved.
There was a tree burning
at the center of your life,
and in bed you found what you loved
was watching the light
fade from someone
else's eyes. It's the body, in the end,
that triumphs over love. And along
with the muffled murmur of pearls,
you'll come to wear your mourning.

Trazada senda

Bañado de luz, el camino
se desvanece
en la curva
donde la luna
deslava
las piedras.
La herida del árbol
es ese instante
de viento. Distintas
intensidades de luz
congregan
mi memoria
inconsistente
como esa estación desnuda
se repliega
hacia
el corazón de mi llaga.

Worn Path

Light-bathed, the road
fades
at the curve
where the moon
bleaches
the stones.
The tree's injury
is just an instant
of wind. Different
intensities of light
draw together
my discordant
memories
as the naked season
contracts
into
the heart of my wound.

Hambre

Es de día en el pueblo de los pescadores.

La sangre fresca de las lubinas
escurre por los esqueletos

como un estallido de jazmines en primavera.
Mas no son flores lo que tus ojos ven.

Es el callado abrirse y cerrarse
de las bocas de los pescados
lo que disemina su muerte.

Sientes náusea, una náusea paradójica
te recubre de la misma escarcha.

La salpicadura en las vitrinas
aviva el tumulto de los mares.

Cuando te destripan el pescado delante de ti,
lo único que ves son las vísceras.

Aun así, ruegas para que el hambre
preserve la luz de tus pupilas.

Hunger

It's daybreak in the fishing village.

The fresh blood of sea bass
slops down through torn

baskets in bursts like spring jasmine.
But it's not flowers that catch your eye.

It's the mute opening and closing
of the fishes' mouths
that broadcasts their death.

You feel nausea, a paradoxical nausea
stiffening you like frost.

The splashing of the fish in glass tanks
simulates the tumult of the seas.

When the fish are gutted in front of you,
all you can see is the viscera.

And still you beg that your hunger
might sharpen the light in your eyes.

Levedad

El amor es una puerta callada,
árbol / tormenta / féretro
fuera del tiempo.

Creamos la idea de un hogar:
la encendida lumbrera,
el libro en el buró.

Toda imagen es real
salvo el jazmín
en llamas.

Lightness

Love is a silent door,
tree / storm / coffin
beyond time.

We invent the idea of home:
the glowing lamp,
the book on the nightstand.

Every image is real
but for that jasmine
in flames.

Tres piedades por Ezra Pound

Rasgadura

Fluye el río, mas no tu voz.
Tu palabra, espejo de inconsciencias, llama
herida a la flor.
De anchuroso caudal, yegua blanca
es el tiempo del aluvión.
Pero el río nunca vuelve.
Por un
instante
tu ojo
rasga
el velo
de la realidad.

Three Devotions for Ezra Pound

Piercing

The river flows on, but not your voice.
Your words, in that mirror of your mind,
confuse the flower for a lesion.
A flood can whirl in every direction
like a frightened mare.
But the river never returns.
Just for an
instant maybe
your eye
pierced
the veil
of the real.

La nieve arde

1.
Si digo bello no hablo de ti, dios de la lengua.
Tampoco del elfo añil en el estanque.
Si digo bello hablo de la luz
de tus ojos que han visto la belleza
flotar en el lago, del cisne negro cuando nombra
las soledades del amor, las soledades de dolor.
Hablo del amor que en la estancia resplandece,
de la plata vieja sobre la consola de una casa vieja,
porque el tiempo hace hablar en nosotros las sombras.

2.
Un bosque se abre y su verdor
me lleva a la duración
de aquellos ojos que un vez amé.
La nieve arde dentro del sueño.

3.
He perdido el hábito de avergonzarme:
mi deseo va hacia las venas del follaje.
Después, esperar el hielo, largas noches de invierno
y el crujir de leños sitiados por el cobalto de la flama.

The Burning Snow

1.

If I say gorgeous, I'm not alluding to you, god of language.
Nor to some indigo elf in the pond.
If I say gorgeous, I'm speaking of the light
in your eyes and of the way they tracked beauty
as it floated on the lake, of the black swans that know
the solitudes of love, the solitudes of longing.
I'm speaking of love that shimmered in this very room,
of some old silver on the credenza in an old house,
because time spurs the shadows within us to speak.

2.

A forest opens and its green
recalls to me the ongoingness
of a pair of eyes I once loved.
Snow burns inside the dream.

3.

I've lost the habit of feeling shame:
my desire shoots through the veins of foliage.
What's to come: waiting for the ice, long winter nights,
and crackling logs besieged by cobalt flames.

Trinità dei Monti

*Cuando el peso de la vida cansa tu cuerpo, cuando tu
corazón se debilita como una hoja de cilantro, cuando hasta
tu cabello se deshace como los pelos del elote, cuando necesitas
que alguien segue las gotas de sangre en tus pies, cuando tu
rostro aún tiene que ser sostenido por la mano de tu madre
y el eco de las injurias se escucha en cada astilla de tu leño,
entonces yo me pregunto cómo es posible que, ante el frío del
mundo, no pueda mirar el púrpura de la sandía, cómo no
percibir la agraciada circunferencia de la manzana, cómo no
escuchar la cantata desde el coro que alberga la deposición
original de tu dolor.*

Roma, junio 21, 2019

Trinità dei Monti[5]

*When life's weight wears down your body, when your heart
withers like a coriander leaf, when even your hair comes
out like corn silk, when you need someone to wipe away the
blood on your feet, when your face still asks to be held in your
mother's hands and the echo of insults vibrates in each splinter
of your wood, then I ask how, given the world's coldness, how
it's possible to see the watermelon's purple, or perceive the
apple's shapely circumference, or hear the choir's cantata in
which the signal deposition of your pain has been recorded.*

Rome, June 21, 2019

Oleaje

Los párpados del sueño se separan.

Llave de otra edad el polvo blancuzco en la semilla.

¿Qué es abandonar la tierra?

Juntos, inferimos alguna semejanza.

Mar adentro del mar, la aserradura, la luz de la estrella y su naufragio.

Luna fragmentada.

Vacío, tu espíritu se hunde en el pozo.

¿Era nuestro el lanzar la piedra, comer del fruto, arrojar el vástago a la acequia?

Lo que en verdad poseemos es sólo–¿qué?

Contra el espejo, la lluvia cae sobre el oleaje gris.

¿Cómo acallar los ecos muy dentro de mi piel?

¿Dónde mi yo y dónde el tú hacia el cual avanzo?

Heavy Swell

Sleep's eyelids part.

The key to another age in the seed's white powder.

To abandon the earth, what does that mean?

Together, we infer a resemblance.

An ocean within the ocean, the deep cut, the star's light and
its collapse.

Fragmented moon.

Emptied out, your spirit sinking into the well.

Was it our given—to throw the stone, to eat of the fruit, to
cast the stem into the ditch?

What's truly ours is only—what?

In the mirror, rain falls over gray waves.

How to silence the echoes beneath the skin?

Where's my I and where the you I approach?

El mundo y sus pliegues infinitos. Trato de acallar el ruido.

No he logrado establecer una relación con lo otro.

¿Dónde refugiarme, dónde la voz que a mí regresa?

Una puerta se abre

hacia atrás e insiste en entrever gestos que no me reconocen:

el instante mira doblemente en el espejo.

Cigüeñas y ánsares encienden mis ojos, preparan mi espíritu.

Con el tiempo hasta el sol debe morir.

El aire tibio del cielo

derrama su agua sobre la raíz

hacia donde camino, tambaleante, en el ocaso.

The world and its countless folds. I tamp down the noise.

I have yet to establish my relationship with the other.

Where to take refuge, where the voice that returns to me?

A door opens

backwards, offering glimpses of gestures that don't recognize
     me:

in the mirror, the instant does a double take.

Storks and geese light up my eyes and ready my spirit.

In time to come, even the sun must die.

The sky's sultry air

empties its water over the roots of things

where, at dawn, I now find myself stumbling.

Tinta

La escritura es
invisible. Eso
que ves en la página
tan sólo es tinta,
espina
blanqueada por el sol.

Aunque retiene la forma del pez,
su rastro es
un signo.
Una arteria dilatada.

Nada
en oscura superficie:
derrubia vertientes
en la precipitación
de las arenas.

Cordón entre guijarros,
te arrastrará, sin nunca
desvelar nuestro sino.

Previously unpublished

Ink

Writing is
invisible. Whatever
you see on the page
is no more than ink,
a sun-bleached
spine.

Though it retains the fish's form,
its ghost song
is a sign.
A dilated artery.

Nothing's
really there
but dark surface:
meltwater slopes
undercut
by windblown sand.

A piece of string
pulled along between pebbles
leads us forward without revealing our fate.

Abandono I

Saliste corriendo por la playa como potranca desbocada.
Tus gafas se quedaron flotando bajo la luna.
Tomé el auto, y me fui al hotel.

Al llegar me asomé por la ventana, pero no regresaste.
Nunca regresaste. Aunque por la mañana nos dimos los
    buenos días
como si nada hubiera ocurrido.

Como si al correr lejos de mí, tu cuerpo lastimado
    lastimándome se hubiera ido
para siempre.

Abandonment 1

You took off down the beach like a runaway colt.
Your glasses, left behind, glinted in the moonlight.
I started the car, drove to the hotel.

When I got there, I stared out the window, but you didn't
    come back.
You never really came back. Although the next day we said
    good morning
like nothing had happened.

It was as though in running from me, your damaged body,
    damaging me, left me
forever.

Abandono VI

La habitación está hecha de pequeños instantes que
  llamamos recuerdos.
En cuál de ellos detenerse es asunto de quien contemple las
  violetas.
Una flor sola puede discordar del universo entero sin
  marchitarse.

Los especialistas en el amor suelen llamar a ese instante
  amor-recuerdo.
Aquella mañana en el hotel aprendí que la primera desnudez
  nos deja en
el desamparo para siempre. Que vivimos toda una vida
  buscando cobijo.

Un conjunto de violetas frente a la ventana puede ser un
  círculo de gracia
en nuestra divagación. Ser santo o mártir conlleva
  abandono. Esto es, salir
desbocados sobre la arena de la playa hacia ningún lugar
  conlleva desentrañar

lo que los filósofos llaman perder rumbo y los científicos
  abandonar la órbita.
Seamos serios cuando hablemos del amor. Pensemos que es
  el síntoma
inscrito en el cuerpo como recordación, mancha, fruto,
  umbral, fresca sed.

Abandonment 6

The room is made of small instants we call memories.
Whoever contemplates violets has to decide on which one
    she'll focus her gaze.
A single flower can upend the whole universe.

Specialists in love usually call this instant love-memory.
On that morning at the hotel, I came to understand the first
    nakedness leaves us
vulnerable forever. That we live a lifetime searching for
    shelter.

A cluster of violets outside the window can describe a circle
    of grace, some relief
from our digressions. Being a saint or martyr requires
    abandonment. Which is
to say, taking off down the beach to nowhere, as you did,
    involves an unraveling,

what philosophers call losing one's way and scientists call
    jumping your orbit.
Let's be serious when we talk about love. Let's understand it
    as a symptom
inscribed in the body as remembrance, stain, fruit, raw
    thirst.

de *Amonites*, Seis

★

Misterio este nacer donde la luz alumbra el árbol de la
muerte.

★

Me pertenece sólo lo que conozco; a lo otro, pertenezco.

★

Temo el rostro que con retazos de incerteza he inventado.

★

No pule el agua la piedra sino la visión del pez.

★

El arte, esa súplica de ciego.

★

No se extravía en el ocaso la gaviota, a su áspera llamada
responden las crestas del mar.

★

En cada página del libro se abre una luz, casi imperceptible
pero siempre luz.

★

Transcurre, no discurre, la espiral sosegada del amonites.

★

This mysterious birth, where light illuminates the tree of
   death.

★

Only what I know belongs to me; to the rest, I belong.

★

I fear the face I've invented out of scraps of uncertainty.

★

The water doesn't polish the stone so much as the fishes'
   vision.

★

Art, the supplication of the blind.

★

The gull doesn't lose itself in twilight, its harsh call is
   answered by crests of swell.

★

On each of the book's pages a light opens, almost
   imperceptible but always light.

★

The serene spiral of the ammonite transpires, it isn't acquired.

★

Llora mi corazón cuando migran las aves, todas las posibilidades del no retorno se arremolinan en mi pecho.

★

Cuando amor no encuentro sé que es tan real que lo he tenido.

★

No te das cuenta de que el líquido rubí es mi sola vida suspendida de ese único sorbo.

★

Por el silbo de la sierpe, pude la sierpe, presiente la arena el agitado cierzo.

★

El dolor humaniza la raíz de las cosas.

★

Hay una tranquila certeza al cerrar el libro que la madrugada, con su estertor crepitante, desvanece.

★

Sucede que escribimos con una tinta que las más de las veces sentimos ajena, aun al releernos.

★

Un mundo sin arte no puede ser pensado.

★

My heart pangs when the birds migrate, the possibilities that they won't return swirl in my chest.

★

When I'm loveless, I'm sure love is real because I know what it is.

★

With one sip of ruby liquid, my life is suspended.

★

From just the hiss of the snake, I could sense sand, the agitated wind.

★

Pain humanizes the root of things.

★

Closing the book with the quiet certainty that dawn, with its crepitant death rattle, will fade into day.

★

So it happens that we write with an ink that, more often than not, looks foreign to us, even as we re-read it.

★

A world without art, unthinkable.

★

No hay final, nunca termina, este silencio es lo blanco
siempre renaciendo.

★

Vamos en pos de un mismo fruto cuya raíz no ha sido aún
plantada.

★

Con cuánta frecuencia la luz de la palabra se opaca en la
tinta.

★

Cuando callo, siento el silencio rojo de la araña contar los
hilos de mis sueños.

★

En espiral volví a donde el tiempo.

★

There is no end, it never ends, this silence is a fresh
   white page.

★

We're searching for the same fruit whose root has yet to
   be planted.

★

So often, the writer's ink only darkens the light of the word.

★

When I fall quiet, I sense the red silence of that spider
   counting the threads of my dreams.

★

I spiral back to where time begins, once again.

NOTES

1. "Sky of Shadows": Samara is the feminine name of a Hebrew guardian spirit; the name means "protected by God."

2. "Ekphrasis": The poet Paul Celan was born Paul Antschel. Celan's poem "Death Fugue" was the inspiration for Anselm Kiefer's painting titled "Sulamith."

3. From *All before Night*, "In your eyes": The Processional Street (Aj-ibur-shapu, meaning "May the invisible enemy not prevail") extended north from the Ishtar Gate and was designed with brick relief images of lions, the animal companion of Ishtar, the goddess of love and war; the dragon of Marduk, the lord of the gods; and the bull of Adad, the storm god. Long stretches of the decorated street's course can still be seen in Babylon.

4. "Fasting": Ahmed Hasim (1884–1933) was a Modernist-Symbolist Turkish writer.

5. "Trinità dei Monti": Trinity of the Mounts is a prominent sixteenth-century Roman Catholic church atop the Spanish Steps in Rome.

Poems Under Saturn: Poèmes saturniens, by Paul Verlaine, translated and with an introduction by Karl Kirchwey

Final Matters: Selected Poems, 2004–2010, by Szilárd Borbély, translated by Ottilie Mulzet

Selected Poems of Giovanni Pascoli, translated by Taije Silverman with Marina Della Putta Johnston

After Callimachus: Poems, by Stephanie Burt, with a foreword by Mark Payne

Dear Ms. Schubert: Poems by Ewa Lipska, translated by Robin Davidson and Ewa Elżbieta Nowakowska, with a foreword by Adam Zagajewski

The Translator of Desires, by Muhyiddin Ibn ʻArabi, translated by Michael Sells

Cantigas: Galician-Portuguese Troubadour Poems, translated and introduced by Richard Zenith

The Owl and the Nightingale: A New Verse Translation, translated by Simon Armitage

Brief Homage to Pluto, by Fabio Pusterla, selected and translated by Will Schutt

A Kiss for the Absolute: Selected Poems of Shuzo Takiguchi, translated by Mary Jo Bang and Yuki Tanaka

Even Time Bleeds: Selected Poems, by Jeannette L. Clariond, translated and introduced by Forrest Gander

† Out of print

GPSR Authorized Representative: Easy Access System Europe - Mustamäe tee 50, 10621 Tallinn, Estonia, gpsr.requests@easproject.com